AF270365

GOATs IN SPORTS

FOOTBALL GOATs

KENNY ABDO

Fly!
An Imprint of Abdo Zoom
abdobooks.com

abdobooks.com

Published by Abdo Zoom, a division of ABDO, P.O. Box 398166, Minneapolis, Minnesota 55439. Copyright © 2025 by Abdo Consulting Group, Inc. International copyrights reserved in all countries. No part of this book may be reproduced in any form without written permission from the publisher. Fly!™ is a trademark and logo of Abdo Zoom.

Printed in the United States of America, North Mankato, Minnesota.
052024
092024

Photo Credits: Alamy, AP Images, Getty Images, Icon Sportswire, Shutterstock
Production Contributors: Kenny Abdo, Jennie Forsberg, Grace Hansen
Design Contributors: Candice Keimig, Neil Klinepier

Library of Congress Control Number: 2023948518

Publisher's Cataloging-in-Publication Data

Names: Abdo, Kenny, author.
Title: Football GOATs / by Kenny Abdo
Description: Minneapolis, Minnesota : Abdo Zoom, 2025 | Series: GOATs in sports |
    Includes online resources and index.
Identifiers: ISBN 9781098285654 (lib. bdg.) | ISBN 9781098286354 (ebook) |
    ISBN 9781098286705 (Read-to-me eBook)
Subjects: LCSH: Football--Juvenile literature. | Football players--Juvenile literature. |
    Football--Records--United States--Juvenile literature. | Professional athletes-
    Juvenile literature.
Classification: DDC 796.332--dc23

TABLE OF CONTENTS

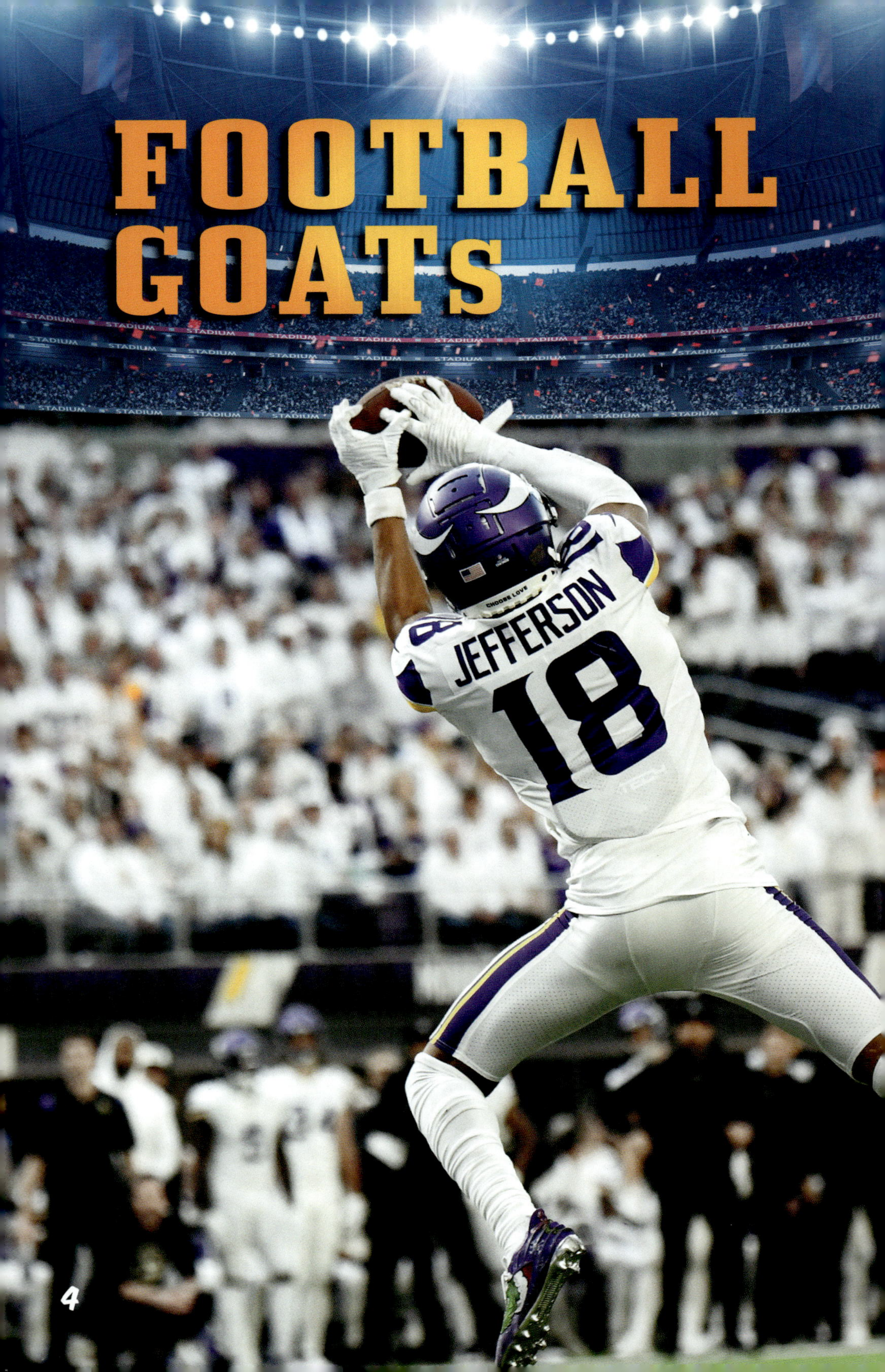

FOOTBALL GOATs

Going long for more than 100 years, the National Football League (NFL) has a bench full of incredible athletes!

SUPER BOWL
SUPER BOWL
LV
TAMPA BAY BUCCANEERS
CHAMPIONS
SUPER BOWL LV
SUPER BOWL LV

With amazing records and exciting **Super Bowl** wins, these football greats have inspired many to go for the extra point!

THE GREATS

Jim Thorpe was more than a **Hall-of-Fame**-worthy football player. He was the NFL's first president from 1920 to 1921. Thorpe also shined in major league baseball and was a two-time **Olympic** gold medalist!

9

Jim Brown never missed a game in his incredible nine seasons with the Cleveland Browns. As a running back, Brown had more than 12,000 rushing yards and three **MVPs**! He made the **Hall of Fame** in 1971.

Dick Butkus was one of the NFL's best linebackers. In his nine seasons with the Chicago Bears, Butkus intercepted 22 passes and recovered 27 fumbles. He was entered into the **Hall of Fame** in 1979.

Joe Montana accomplished a lot in his 14 years with the San Fransisco 49ers. He nabbed four **Super Bowl** wins and was **MVP** in three of them. The **QB** rightfully earned the nickname, "Joe Cool."

Walter Payton was the NFL's all-time leading rusher throughout his career. After his death, the NFL renamed the Man of the Year Award the Walter Payton NFL Man of the Year Award.

Wide receiver Jerry Rice worked hard for his nickname "The GOAT." He earned three **Super Bowl** rings with the 49ers. Rice also holds numerous NFL records that may never be broken!

Peyton Manning is one of the greatest **QBs** of all time. He has won two **Super Bowls** and earned a record five **MVP** Awards. Manning made the **Hall of Fame** in 2021.

Tom Brady changed the game in his 22 seasons. He nabbed seven **Super Bowl** wins. That is the most Super Bowl wins for any player. It is also more wins than any NFL team!

Patrick Mahomes reached GOAT status very quickly. As the Kansas City Chiefs **QB**, he helped his team win the **Super Bowl** in the 2019, 2022, and 2023 seasons! Mahomes was crowned **MVP** all three times.

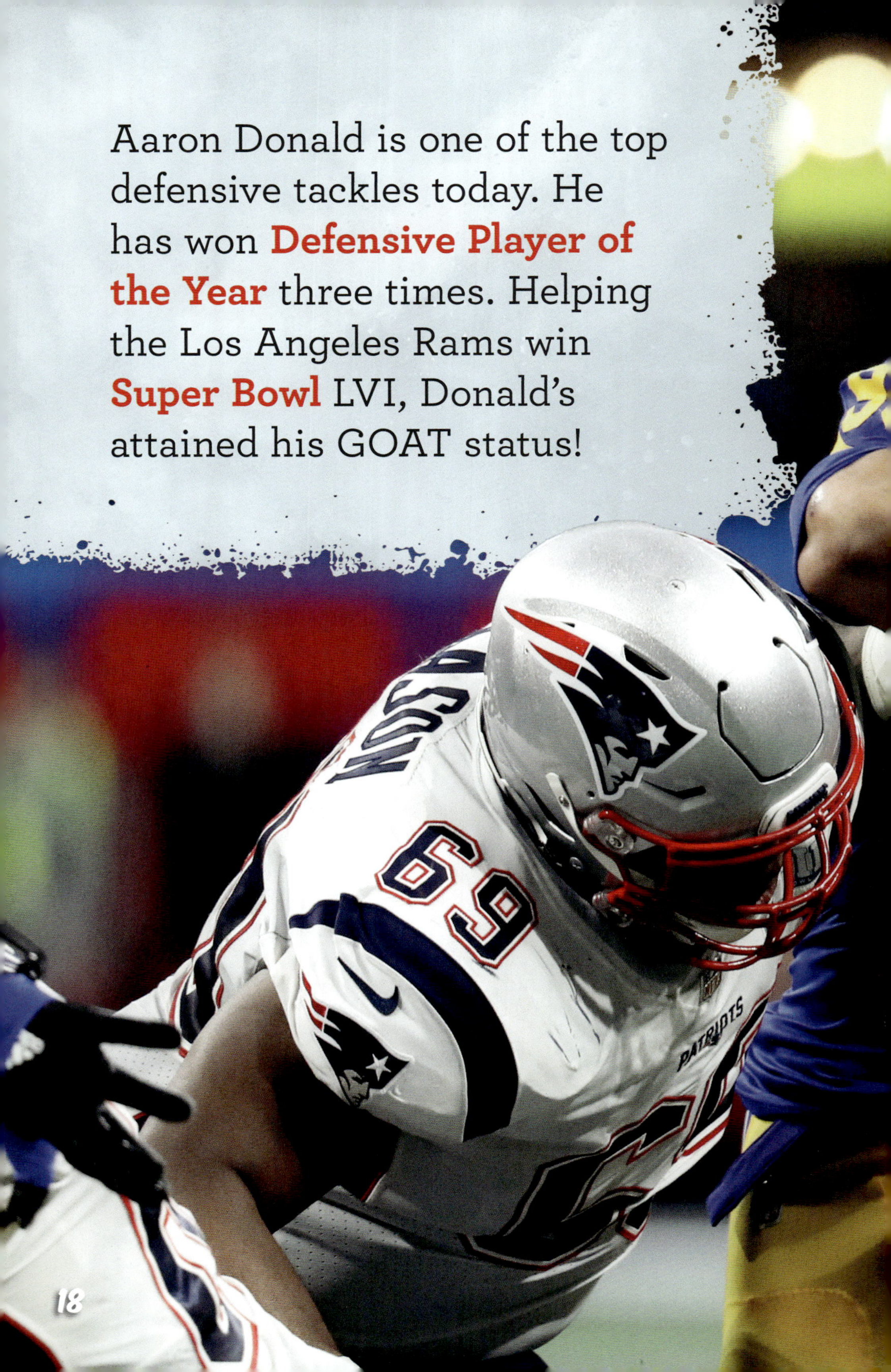

Aaron Donald is one of the top defensive tackles today. He has won **Defensive Player of the Year** three times. Helping the Los Angeles Rams win **Super Bowl** LVI, Donald's attained his GOAT status!

SCOREBOARD

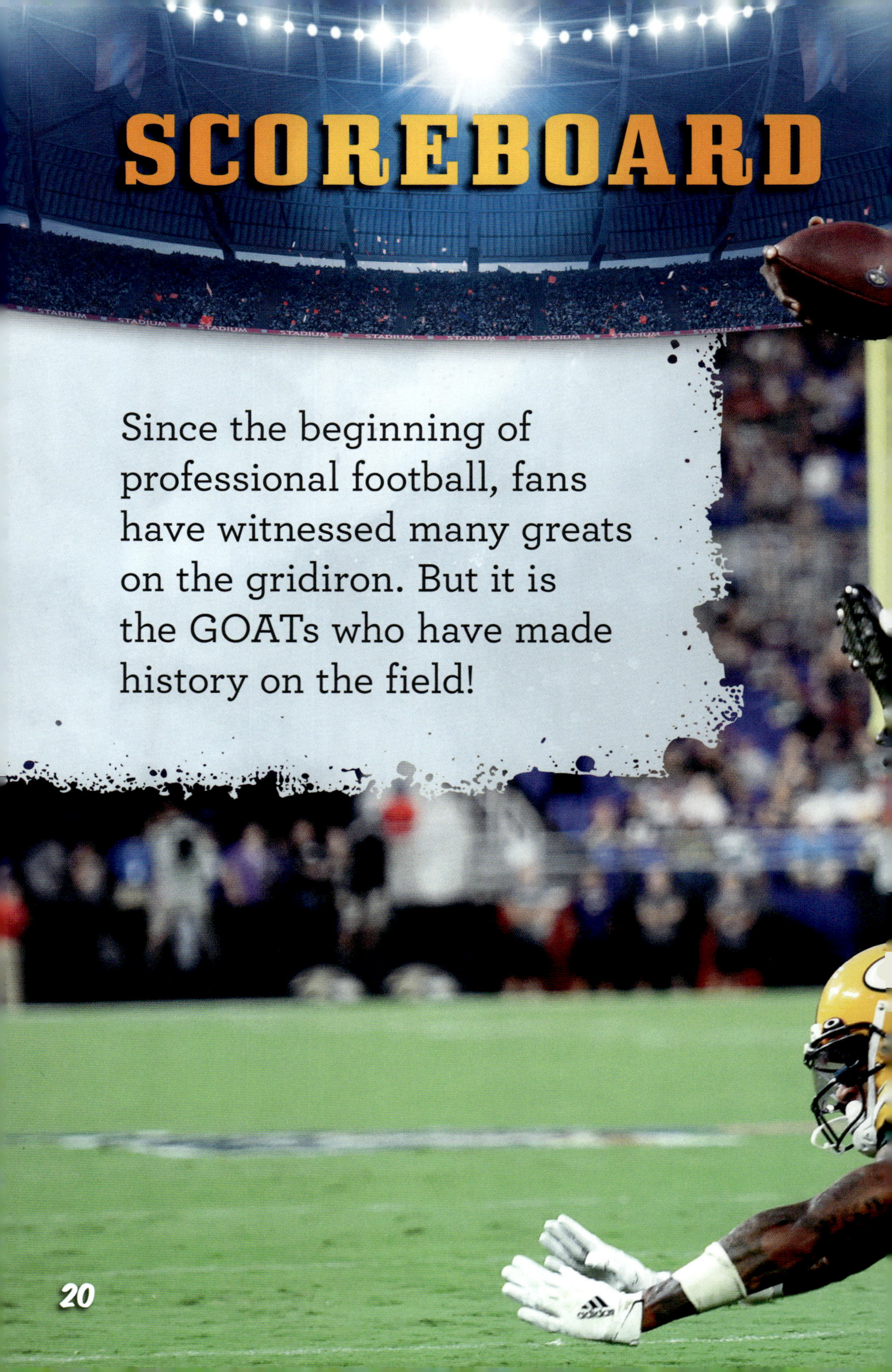

Since the beginning of professional football, fans have witnessed many greats on the gridiron. But it is the GOATs who have made history on the field!

GLOSSARY

Defensive Player of the Year – an award given by the Associated Press to the most outstanding defensive player in the NFL at the end of every season.

Hall of Fame – the group of highly celebrated people honored for their achievements in a sport or other activity. In football, it is called the Pro Football Hall of Fame.

MVP – short for "most valuable player," an award given in sports to a player who has performed the best in a game or series.

Olympic – of or relating to the Olympic Games. The Games are the biggest international athletic events held as separate winter and summer competitions every four years in a different city.

QB – short for quarterback, the player on the offensive team who directs teammates in their play.

Super Bowl – the NFL championship game, played once a year.

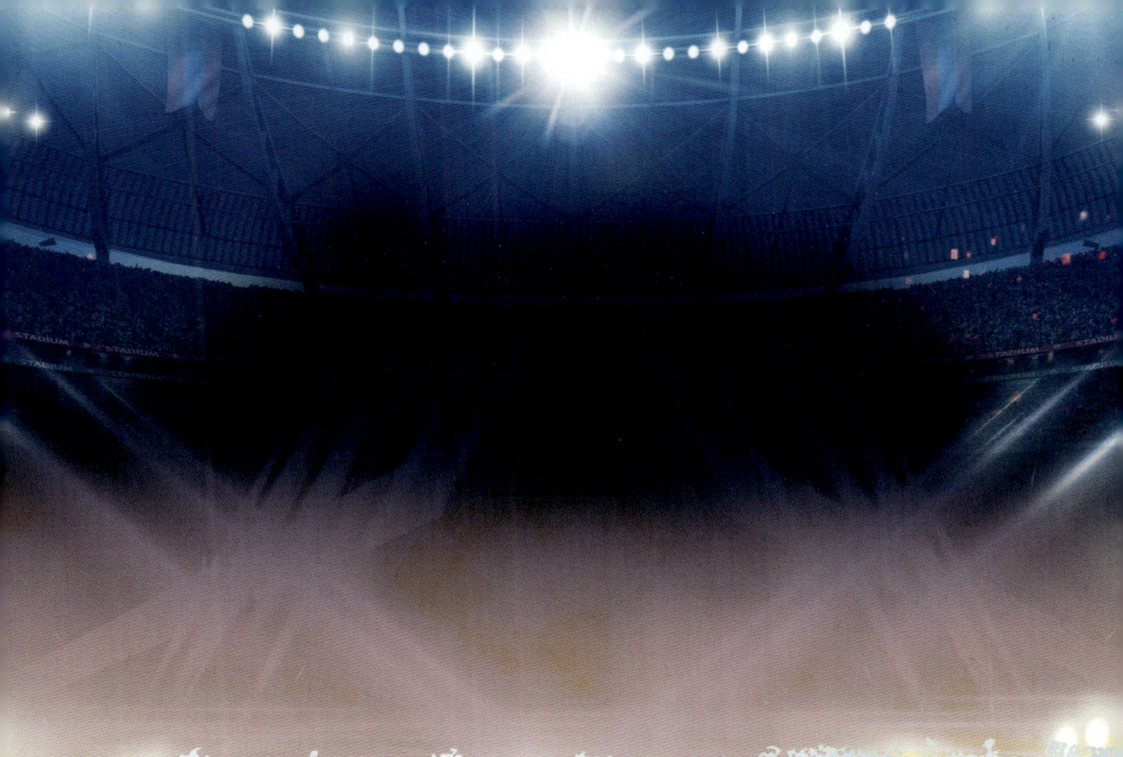

ONLINE RESOURCES

To learn more about the GOATs in Football, please visit **abdobooklinks. com** or scan this QR code. These links are routinely monitored and updated to provide the most current information available.

INDEX